When will you let yourself see?

[of questions and answers on identity]

By Oriana Jemide

1. Eden
2. What Do You Do With Wounds?
3. Free Man
4. Breaking Bad Habits Begins With Belief
5. The Shift
6. Tomorrow. Today.
7. From A Conversation About 'The Struggle'
8. The Breaking
9. On Healing: Facing Things Head On
10. What Do You Do When Your Victory Ends?
11. If You Will Only
12. On Healing: Practising Stillness
13. How To Be Before God
14. Sins of the Father [against sons]
15. On Connection
16. Hands.
17. Of Light and Strength.
18. What Is The Truth? [There is help for the helpless]
19. What Do You Do You

When You Don't Feel like Forgiving
20. The Art of Watching and Waiting I
21. Sins of the Father [against daughters]
22. Feet.
23. Sometimes The Shame Comes Back.
24. The Art of Watching and Waiting II
25. What Is The Truth? [The pure in heart will see God]
26. On Accountability
27. Of Salt and Being Seasoned
28. Bloodline.
29. From His Heart To Whom It May Concern
30. The Art of Watching and Waiting III
31. Journey.

For anyone who feels stuck, lost, burdened by life's many trials. I hope you find a glimmer of hope as you flick through the pages of this book.

May you find truths you can hold onto, truths that affirm you, truths that carry you for days to come.

- Oriana

1. Eden

Eden is not a lost place
It is found
Face down
Heart wide open

If you let go of the pain
You are feeding fresh fruits
You will find
That Eden is in you
You are Eden.

2. What Do You Do With Wounds?

What do you do with wounds?
What do you do with wounds that won't heal?

Are you not tired of the band-aid?
Sealing your sores with the short lived
safety-net of the overnight drink,
the company of men?

Quick fixes do not serve you

Are you not tired of beating your head against
brick walls?
Are you not tired of beating your head against
the brick walls of homes you don't belong?
Is it worth the concussion for a short term
stay in a flat in another man's name
When you have been given a nation?
Why do you fight for rations
When you have a feast awaiting your return?
Why do you turn and turn and turn…
Why must you move
Why does stillness unsettle you?

Is it because you will have to dine with the
truth?

Are you not tired of sealing shattered
ornaments in your temple with pva glue
When you could just make room?
why does space unsettle you?

Is it because you may have to let go of the
familiar for fresh fruits?

Why do you slave over the ground to plant

seeds when you have inherited a garden of
fresh fruits?
You prefer to be puffed up by the praise for
work than to be nourished by your inheritance
Why do you take the stance of slave
When you could just surrender?
Pay for sacrifices when you could just submit?

The strength in your sacrifice is not in price
that you pay but how much of yourself you give
with it

Are you not tired of clenched fist and bruised
knuckles?
Why do you fight against yourself?
Why do you cry to be released then stand in
the way of your own healing?
Why do you pray for fire if you runaway every
time it tries to burn away
what you fight so hard to overcome?
Why do you run and run and run…
Why don't you just stand still?
Stay long enough to drop the act
Long enough to unpack the bags you have
dragged around town
From pillar to post you straddle around like a
ghost, no more meat on your bones
Because you have berated your flesh so much
that you have choked your spirit
Stay long enough for your tears to become the
water that washes over your wounds
Long enough for it to sting
Stinging may be uncomfortable but it is safe
Will you stay long to be safe
To be strengthened
To be open

What do you do with wounds that won't heal?

Will you open your wounds?
Let scars shows, will you walk even with the limp in your step
Will you surrender?

Surrender is the solution that safeguards and strengthens.

3. Free Man

You pray against stagnancy
but simultaneously build a temple for
your pain
And preach it from the pulpit
As though it was testimony

You testify to your brokenness
As though it was a prize
You compete with your fellow man
Over who has endured the most suffering
As though it was proof of your value
But what does it profit a man to lose his
soul
And gain the world

The world being - the need for validation
Through sing songs of your slavery
The cheering and throwing of confetti at
your pity party
You have made a monument of pity
And hung it from your ceiling
It is the first thing you see
When you rise early in the morning
You kneel at its and soon after
You are clothed with victim
You crown yourself with rage and claim it
is okay because it is righteous

You have turned a season of struggle into
your story
Do you even know who you are outside of
sorrow?
Or have you so romanticized bitterness
that

You can no longer tell the difference between
Egypt and the Promised Land

Do you only know how to lift your hands in the
sanctuary of your flaws?
Your imperfections - Baal,
So now you produce fruits of lack
You have nothing
Because you have called yourself nothing
You have forgotten your name and laid with
blame
Never needing nurture
You have forgotten who you are outside of
torture

That you give the Earth its taste
Your granules eliminate the mild
Making matter out of waste
You illuminate the dark places with your
presence
Placing praise on the tongues of pain stricken
people

You make prophets
Whose posture is tall and straight
Because they are no longer wearing
The weight of a ten thousand slaves

Do you know that your name is - Chosen
Your appointment, a series of fortunate event
Your snicket may be narrow but it is secure
So stop spewing your synthetic modesty and
call it humility
The humble are lowly of heart
And singing songs of your slavery as sonnets
Is low in self - image

Remember that your name is - Chosen

And the hairs on your head are counted
Your season in chains are not your calling
You are no longer captive
You are clothed
And shame is not your uniform
Your name is Free Man
So why are you still fighting for freedom?

4. Breaking Bad Habits Begins With Belief

On my journey of identity, the concept of faith is becoming more real to me. I am learning that my reality does not define who I am and in a world that has a mind of "that's just how it/he/she is" or "that's just how it/he/she has always been", it can be hard! I am now knowing what it fully means to 'believe in what is unseen' when it comes to me and those around me. I can no longer join in the cynicism or hopelessness of the world, if I want to bring hope to the world. I have had to break up with hopelessness and choose to take on only what is good, pure, admirable and so on, even when it has not been my reality. You can only become what you believe about yourself, every bit of doubt is counter-productive to the you, you envision and the change you want to see in the world.

Changing the world around you begins with you. The problem we often encounter as people is we try to work from the outside in, we try to fix, save, address the brokenness around us without first addressing our own and then changing our perspective on the state of the world. It is easy to scream 'I am not of this world, I am on my wave' but that will only show through how you approach the world. 'Cancelling' the world or this generation makes you just as 'bad' as the world you want to change. You must choose to see light where there is darkness, that is what faith is! But it starts with you! The world is like a mirror, if you can only ever see the negative, it is a reflection of your belief system.

To break away from negative actions, you must break away from negative thought patterns, to break away from negative thought patterns, you must renounce the old and adopt new ones (especially when they are not your reality).

HOW DO YOU SPEAK ABOUT YOURSELF TO YOURSELF AND TO OTHERS? (This is a great place to start)

5. The Shift

Formerly: a creature of habit
Now you are shedding skin
To make room for new wine
Festivals of hope
I hope that you will no longer pigeon-hole yourself
With tales of your trauma
I invite you to move on
Will you move on?

6. Tomorrow. Today.

Self-confidence looks like pride
To the one whose eyes are fixated on everyone but themselves

Will you turn your gaze
Will you let yourself see yourself for who you truly are
Or will you continue to find comfort in the company
Of those who are blinded by comparing
Their second chapter to another's finished article

There is no humility in hiding
Hiding your glory for the sake of not becoming your own god
Is it better to worship anxiety?
Do you not see how you have made a god out of your inability to finish?
You claim you do not want to steal from the one that made you
As you bury your gift in the ground
Do you hear that sound?
Claps calling you into the spotlight
Will you ignore it one more time

'I will start tomorrow'

Do you even know if you will see tomorrow?
Do you not see how you have made a god out of tomorrow
Tomorrow. Tomorrow. Tomorrow.
Tomorrow is borrowed time.

Will you taste and see the fruitfulness of

today?
Will you drink from the well today?
Will you water the seed today?
Will you stay to watch it sprout?
Or will you worship anxiety again?

Rinse and repeat. Today.
Will you wake up from your sleep today?
Will you open your eyes to your shared authority today?
Or will you let tomorrow take centre stage one more time?

Rinse and repeat. Today.
Will you wake up from your sleep today?
Firm, filter, fasten your feet today?
It would be a shame if someone else ran your race.

7. From A Conversation About 'The Struggle'
—

Why must we be raised on struggle and survival?
Work twice as hard to get only half of what they have?
Who said it must be so?
Why do we continue to relive the story that many died for, to die with them?
Stories. History. I wonder if we are wasting time finding erased history…
Shouldn't we just write new stories?
Reality. Why are we so accustomed to a reality that says we will always suffer and still never reach the pinnacle of our glory?
Always. Never. When will we stop using our tongues to tangle ourselves in a web of lies?
Lies. Why are we better versed in the lies of doubt and defeat?
Defeat. Does it not bother you that your first thought is one of defeat?
Reality.
Why are you so accustomed to the reality that struggle defines you?
Struggle. I stand to see the day that you will know yourself outside of struggle.
Struggle.

I stand to see the day that you will know you outside of chains, whips and wounds
Struggle.
I stand to see the day that you will stop striving, stop surviving, stop measuring your strength by

your suffering
Struggle.

I stand to see the day that you will see
yourself in high places, safe spaces,
Struggle. Spaces. Faces. That your face will
exist amongst other faces for you are worth
being seen.
Seen. Struggle.
Slavery.
**I stand to see the day that your story will
not begin and end with slavery**
**I stand to see the day that your story will
not begin and end with slavery**
**I stand to see the day that your story will
not begin and end with slavery.**

8. The Breaking

Weeping:

I know that you hate to cry
but you must
That is how you serve notice to pain
That is how your home makes room for new tenants
That rise at the crack of morning
To make meals that strengthen your bones

Lamenting;

Bones. To serve notice to dry bones
you must call it out, call it by its name
Shame is the silencer
that finds safety on the waist of one
that would lubricate it
Do not get trigger happy
with the thing that will leave you empty

you must call it by its name
because shame only has the power
to take life in secrecy.

9. On Healing: Facing Things Head On

Pursuing healing, emotional or mental is not for the faint-hearted. It takes a lot of courage to face your pain head on, sometimes it's just easier to pretend things never happened. But you see that pain you are so afraid of has a way of coming back and multiplying itself affecting your relationships, character and calling.

So how do you face things head on?

Be honest about your emotional state
The world has a way of preaching things that sound good on paper but do more harm than good in reality. One of them is 'FAKE IT TILL YOU MAKE IT', although this may work for some parts of life, it does not work for you emotional/mental state. HEALING CANNOT HAPPEN WHERE THERE IS PRETENCE. You owning up to brokenness doesn't not define you, it is simply a pit stop on your journey of wholeness.

Be broken but don't stay broken
One thing I have noticed in the current climate is we are very good wallowers. We like to stew in our pain, make the pity party last just a little longer. I would even go as far as saying that we sell our pain; pain is relatable so we want to be the influencer known for having the hardest life, it sells books, gets views and praise. But what happens when that is all you become known for? How

do you move on, redefine yourself? PAIN IS A SEASON NOT YOUR CALLING.

10. What Do You When Victory Ends?

You step foot into the stillness of home
Worn out from the war of working yourself into the ground
Fresh wounds on your wrists, knuckles and fingertips
But you never stay long enough for them to become scabs
The itch to re-enter the battlefield of life precedes healing
You tell yourself that…

'Hands produce hopelessness when in a dormant state'
So you work yourself into the ground, that is your sole source of fulfilment
A status symbol
You would rather be called resilient than be refreshed
You would rather boast of the blisters of burn out than breath

But…

What do you do when your victory ends with the busyness of life?
And you step foot into the stillness of home
Will you be brave enough to face the silence that greets you at the door?
Will you choose the couch over the desk?

Will you choose a cup of tea over coffee?
Or will you dust your insecurities under the carpet once more?

Will you proceed to pillow talk your exhaustion
Snapshot the influx of emails to prove you are the chief of
'When you were sleeping, I was grinding' association
But working yourself into the ground will not save you from the sorrow of your childhood
Burying yourself in business will not hide you from the cloud of heaviness over your head

Face it or stand to repeat the generational cycle.

11. If You Will Only
—
Stop.
Searching for wholeness.
You are complete.

If you will only
Let your roots grow deep
Deep enough to
Reach the source
The world tells you
'Have thick skin'
But tough never tastes the safety
Your soul is searching for

So stop.
Searching.
And still yourself
Enough to let your roots grow deep
Enough to taste the source.
Regardless of reality
You can own your identity
Renounce a mentality of hopelessness
Because you were not made just to survive but
to do exceedingly and abundantly
You are glory - in the flesh

12. On Healing: Practising Stillness

Healing requires stillness, which is perhaps one of the most difficult things to do in such a fast paced world.

How do you practice stillness?

FIND A FIXED TIME AT THE BEGINNING OR END OF YOUR DAY (where there are no distractions) TO MEDITATE AND STRATEGISE
For some people it is early in the morning, for others it is late at night, the point is it is a time where the world stops for a bit. It is in the physical silence that you can build a system that works even in the noise. This is a time to reflect, refresh, rejuvenate and plan the next day or the current day.
As a Christian, I spend my time listening to soaking sounds/instrumentals and going to place with God in my mind, when I come I am ready for my day!

TAKE MOMENTS WITHIN YOUR DAY TO DO THE SAME THING
Doing the morning or night thing is sometimes the easy part, we feel ready for our day but the busyness of the day starts to drain the energy we worked for at the start of the day. You must practice meditating even with the noise. Nothing is stopping you from taking a quick 10 minutes to read over your affirmations, or soak during your lunch break rather that scroll through endless content online. If this is too hard... SET REMINDERS TO MEDITATE OR EVEN WHAT TO MEDITATE ON
I set my affirmations and bible verses for

that season of my life as reminders on my phone, to show up every other hours. So basically I am still for about 5 minutes every two hours and that CONSISTENCY makes all the difference.

13. How To be Before God

open your wounds:
let your scars show
the burnt flesh that is causing a limp in your step
Leaving ashes spread across your bed with more and more nights of unrest
stop.
concealing your distress
submit.
only then can His beauty flow.
break down:
let the tears roll off your eyelids
and into His palms
let the Psalms roll off your tongue
'the troubles of my heart have enlarged
call a truce to this civil war'
let your pain bounce off the walls of your war room
and into the ears of your Bridegroom
lift the veil over your heart and mind
let Him lift the veil over your eyes.

ask confidently:
let your requests be made known
yes He is all-knowing
but where is the intimacy in:
hidden petitions
shielded intercessions
masked child-like questions
He wants the words to move from your heart to your lips
because your speech is victory over the enemy
with each word spoken
the chains of the fear of vulnerability are broken.

listen attentively:
let your mind and your heart
be still
in your stillness there is clarity
in your silence there are answers,
answers to prayers prayed for decades:
a sling shot of peace knocking down every Goliath
a vision of the closed mouth of lions
a deep sleep and dream of your cup running over
a voice of conviction leading you through and out of the valley of the shadow of death
an assurance of His Word, His Truth that tramples upon every lie of the enemy.

laugh a lot:
let the joy of your heart
and excitement on your lips
be a way to commune with Abba
He delights in you with singing
Enjoy Him with laughter
just be.
be yourself.
He knows exactly what you are like
He fashioned you before the foundation of the world
so no part of you can make Him retreat.

14. Sins of the Father [against sons]

I beat my chest
For the one who sees himself through his father's mistakes
Who repeats the chorus his father belted through bruised egos
It appears he only took note when his father's notes were brash
And brutally mutilating women's flesh
He sings in distasteful keys because he never learnt to read the music of ease
Sensitivity unsettles him, unless it's coming from a damsel in distress

I beat my chest
As he only picked up how to run away, roam, read his way through, never completing text
All these unfinished books
He calls them conquests
But doesn't even have the courage to engage in hand to hand combat
That level of intimacy is beyond his capacity to attack
In his defence he was never taught to connect, to comfort, to cascade with love and protection
I hope that today is the last day he will behave like a victim of some form of oppression
As it is causing him to leave victims in his trail
I hope that he will rise from the hail and the dust of dealing the cards life has dealt him
And he will shake off self-service and swim across the oceans of sacrifice
That a lack of self-control will no longer be

how he measures his manhood
And the abuse of his body will not be a cause for celebration
I hope that he will wash out the dirt of degradation from his eyes,
That has been passed on through generations in the form of one-liners

'Men were not made for monogamy, it is simply in our nature to cheat'

I hope that he will renounce such heresy
And hear, taste and see the truth of who he is meant to be

15. On Connection

Sometimes I beat myself up for feeling, for taking risks in relationships, letting people in, then I remember there is no life without that. Society says 'shut people out', 'don't let your guard down' but we were made for connection and connection requires trust and trust is risky.

People think shutting people out or having your guard up is 'having boundaries' but boundaries are healthy things. Boundaries aren't 'I'm not going to connect with people because I've been hurt'. Boundaries mean you get to have connection with respect.
Don't let pain rob you of healthy connections which is a basic human need. Our make-up needs connection and community.

During creation everything was 'very good' to God. **God's first dissatisfaction was that man was alone. You were not made to do life alone.**

16. Hands.

Have you ever looked at them in different way?
Wondered how your life would change if you had none?

Hands have the ability to create or destroy
Build kingdoms
Or steer ships in the wrong direction
Do you ever wonder what end of the spectrum you are on?
Or does it not matter to you?
Are hands just things connected to your arms?
Do you care what they fashion, form, find?

Will you sleep peacefully tonight?
Will you sleep peacefully tonight knowing everything you touched was filled with life?

17. Of Light and Strength

You are light
Illuminating the paths you walk through
Do not let the darkness you've lived through
Creep in and cloud you

You are strength
Lifting the hearts of men with your presence
Do not let the weakness you are living through
Weigh you down and make you wallow in it
        Fix your gaze
        On the pages that make the Word
        In it are words of life...
        Words of light...

You are light
Emitting rays that don't just run through
But reach down to rest...
That resonate
Relieving men of ruthlessness
Readying them for fights that don't require fists
But chests...
        You teach people to live from their hearts
        You instil hope in the helpless
        Helping the heaped heaviness
        Heave it's way out of them

        You soften the blows of life
        You speak words with weight,
        Words of life:
        Easing the discomfort of wounds and weariness
        Weaning them off weak things
        That bring short-lived safety

>   Safely wearing on them wisdom
>   That wields wealth in the flesh and spirit.

You are strength
Because your Source is Strength
So fix your gaze
On the pages of His Word
In it are words of life...
Words of light...
Your light.

18. What is the Truth [there is help for the helpless]

Saying:
God helps those who help themselves

Truth:
Happy and fully satisfied are the
helpless for theirs
is the kingdom of Heaven.

Do not get carried away with the gift of authority.
Its operation is tied to your submission to the One who would see you walk in its fullness.

Your weakness is the place
Strength comes to be born
Will you labour through the pain?

19. What Do You Do When You Don't Feel Like Forgiving?

I know the heat of justice is what boils in your blood
As you observe the peace of the one who wronged you
'An eye for an eye, a tooth for a tooth' is the song that rings in your mind
As you remember the sting their unsavoury words summoned in you
And how their actions left you with missing pieces to your life's puzzle

But believe me when I tell you that you will never find peace
In waiting for karma to knock them
For even when it does you will still be left with wounds unattended
Because you were so caught up in seeking revenge
That you could not see how you had become the new antagonist in your story

How your obsession with vindication dug deeper into the cuts they made
Now you are closer to caving in
And there is nowhere to lay blame
Will you allow yourself begin again?

Justification.
They hurt you. You hurt them. They hurt you again
Does anyone end up justified?
'An eye for an eye, a tooth for a tooth' leaves the world toothless and blind
What is a world without eyes to pierce

through, soften the hearts of men
And voices to break chains off the oppressed?

Captive.
You say you want to be free
Well true freedom is found in your ability to release before an apology
I know that the pain is exhausting,
I know the healing is dragging its feet
But would you please walk with her
At the end of the valley is a table and a cup overflowing
Do not let bitterness stagnate you

You say you want to be free
But will you drink the truth?
It's a bitter pill to swallow
But it heals better than wallowing
Forgiveness feels like foolishness
when wounds are still fresh
But what you feel is not always what justifies the end.

20. The Art of Watching and Waiting I

I know this place feels desolate and outside is pouring with rain but I hope you will be patient enough to see where this takes you.

I am now awake after falling asleep at 6.30am, but what this came to be, was so worth it. I am learning a lot about the art of waiting, of watching and waiting, of resting and waiting. As someone who loves structure, who loves plans, who loves to be in control, it is hard to do life when things you planned are going pear-shaped or not even happening at all.

What do you do when you feel stuck? When you keep trying things and they keep failing? When it becomes so exhausting to try that give up and cave into the sadness that comes not seeing the fruits of what you put in? When you become too tired to try at anything else...eat, sleep, even shower? What happens when you let go and let life happen to you? How do you do realign yourself?

Start by dealing in days. I have always hated the saying "Take things one day at a time", mostly because it has come in attempt to comfort me but I have found no comfort in it being said. However, it has been the greatest comfort as lived experience. Choosing to take daily stock of myself (emotionally, physically and mentally), and working out my needs for the day, has been healing to me. Journal, write how you really feel out (perhaps as a letter to God) then write out what needs to change in question form (Ask Him to help!).

Wait to listen throughout your day.

Get up and go somewhere. A walk. A late night cinema trip. A coffee shop date. The longer you sit indoors with all the junk, the easier it is to stew in it and harder it is to come out.

Pray. I believe strongly in the power of prayer. It has been my greatest struggle on my spiritual journey and it has definitely been hard to do the past few months. What I have learnt in this time about prayer is it's really about getting your rhythm with God. I know you may have learnt a bunch of stuff about how long, how to, where to, when to pray and sometimes it gets in the way. I say lay all of that stuff down and start a video/audio chat with God...yep turn that recording device on and act like you are chatting to your best friend!

21. Sins of the Father [against daughters]

I beat my chest
For the one who sells herself short
Let's her skirt rise to her neck
For a short-lived safety net
I beat my chest in confidence
That she will break up with hopelessness
Stop fishing for company and compliments
And know that she has been made a fisher of men
That she is not just good for bringing life into the world
But bringing life to the world

I beat my chest
Because she has filled her tank with oil instead of water
She has lubricated her flesh
I hope that she will soon come to her senses
And see herself through lenses of holiness
That Purity is not a far-fetched concept
It is an identity
A multi-coloured coat
I hope that she will wear it with confidence
With a spring in her step
And that she will cast her net with faith that in it will return
A fleet of men of honour and dignity

[They are not a dime in a dozens, if your eyes are not clouded with bitterness of your father's absence]

22. Feet.

Blessed is the man who does not walk in the counsel of the wicked.

Will you let your life stop being run
By the advice of those who only bring lies, death and destruction
Packaged as the gift that keeps on giving
Until it doesn't
Stuck
In sinking sand
Because you have worshipped a genie
You have worshipped the god of granting your every wish with one clean sweep
Instead of the God of relationship
You would rather relish in the romance of things
Than be serenaded by the Creator of them

Blessed is the man who does not walk in the counsel of the wicked.
The wicked:

Those who would present a one dimensional being whose sole purpose is to dish out goods
Instead of giving you food that would nourish you for life.

23. Sometimes the Shame Comes Back

sometimes the shame comes back
Sometimes the shame comes back as whispers
from women who you sought wisdom from
Who you called sisters and mothers
Whose comfort was supposed to lather and wash over you

Do you know what it feels like to be spoken about and never spoken to? Never asked 'What are you reacting to? How is this affecting you?'

Sometimes the shame comes back
Sometimes the shame comes back as societal standards spoken ignorantly from the lips of a lover
Have you ever been tongue-lashed by a lover?
Slapped by the silent stare of disdain after you mustered the courage to share
Told that it didn't matter, that they didn't care
Only to have *how could you's* and *what were you thinking's*
Rained down on you
Acidic.
It eats at your already starving flesh
Heavy.
It soaks up every crevice of your heart.

Why didn't I just lie? I could have saved myself another encounter with shame. They say the truth sets you free, why does this truth re-entangled me

What do you do when the things that were

supposed to shelter you, open the door for
shame to sit with you?

Sometimes the shame comes back
As played back memories
Playback. Memories. Playback.
Attacked. Broken. Silenced.

You cannot see anything beyond the stage of
your worst kept sins
Would it be safe to say you cannot see
yourself anymore
You have closed the curtains on dreams, on
vision, on purpose, on purpose

*What can I really do for anyone? Would I not
be a hypocrite telling people how to live when
I am just as broken as the next person? Am I
even worth listening to?*

What do you do when the things that were
supposed to shelter you, open the door for
shame to settle?

Have you ever tried just getting up?
Standing in an open space and screaming the
shame off?
Is that too much?
How about reaching out?
Do you know that shame does its best work when
you isolate
Will your response to *are you okay*, no longer
be *I'm good* but *I feel ashamed*
*How about reflecting on all the good you've
done
Amidst the mistakes are the victories
The lives you've changed, the leaps and bounds*

you've made
This is where you make it count.

24. The Art of Watching and Waiting II

Do you see these trees growing?
At the moment they look like nothing
Just stork and bark
What if I told you that nothingness has an end
That when you come to the end of nothing
The door opens for something new.

Do you see these trees growing?
This is how what you have laboured for night and day
will sprout from the ground and bloom in due season.
Will you watch and wait?

25. What is the Truth [the pure in heart will see God]

Saying:
Fake it, till you make it

Truth:
Happy are those who are pure in heart for they will see God

To be pure in heart is to confess your sins and sorrows How will you heal if you continue to hide
Under the guise of having faith
When you pretend you blind yourself to the blessing of freedom

Will you offload the baggage of old
Or continue to be sold traditional tales
Packaged as religious truth

You want release but refuse to reveal the things that have left you broken

'The devil will hear me and use it against me'
God will also hear you and use it to heal you

Who will you put your faith in?

26. On Accountability

What is it about letting people into the deep, dark parts of you that incites fear? Maybe it's the fact that when you have shared those parts in the past, they have only bred shame and judgement. Could it be that you were sharing your flaws with the wrong people?

I can see how past condemnation has led to you managing your poor choices in isolation to the point that you have now become comfortable with your mistakes. You justify every decision, every action with 'That's just how I am' but I am here to pull the rug from underneath feet and tell you, you are wrong. 'That's how I am' is an excuse that prevents you from being held accountable and what happens when you are not held accountable?

If people are not held accountable, we are allowing them to stay stuck in cycle of negative behaviour that they will transfer through hurt and pass on to others around them. If we let people escape accountability for their poor choices, we are robbing them of the opportunity to be their true selves.
A lack of accountability allows people accept their bad decisions as their identity.

27. Of Salt and Being Seasoned.

Who are you without the praise?
Do you have any bearing of your being
That does not begin and end with accolades?

Refresh page. Refresh page. Refresh.
Four turned five turned ten turned fifty turned a hundred likes.
Are you satisfied?
Will your value always be tied to the taste of validation from voices you have and probably will never meet?

Just five more follows and it will be five thousand
A glorious achievement
But have you spent time finding security beyond subscriber counts
Do you count even when you are not out there influencing culture?
Are you even seasoned enough to share?
Or are you running on a glass half-full to prove you are somebody?

Will you stop for a second, a minute, maybe an hour
Or is that too much time to take care of yourself
You are so busy being selfless to fill some sense of pride
Only the **truly selfless will reap the reward**
Will you stop for a second, a minute, maybe an hour
To stop chasing reward
To deal with rejection
To manage your expectations

To be satisfied
To be satisfied with yourself
Outside the things you do.

28. Bloodline

When will you stop
Excusing your vices?
Blaming it on a childhood not well -lived
As if you have a monopoly on pain

I hope that you
Will stop drinking
From the well of self-pity
And reconcile with the new wine of your royal
bloodline.

29. From His Heart to Whom it May Concern.

On the days it is foggy
And the pain of the year-old wound stings fresh
I hope that you would let the tears burst out of you,
Free flowing, flooding…
Whatever floats the boat of the heaviness you have
Refused to release
I hope that you would at least shed a few tears - for healing begins there

I hope that in your grief you would not put pressure
On yourself to pray
Or force-feed yourself scripture
But you would sit still and picture green pastures

I know you are restless
And there is a wrestle in you to overcome this in a sort of warfare
But if you would just reach out and hold My hand
Just let Me lead, let Me lead you
You will see that this battle can happen with ease
If you would just…
If you would just walk with Me
You will see that it is not about running with speed
If you would just slow down enough to glide
You would notice the beauty of the trees that are yet to bloom
Because you would have stayed long enough
to envision and soak up the future
Instead of fussing and stumbling to get there.

30. The Art of Watching and Waiting
III

Winter is coming and you are yearning for spring again
But are you ready to begin again?
Are you ready for uncomfortable tendencies
And uncharted territory?
Does blooming bother you
If it means parting ways with what you once thought was here to stay?

31. Journey

In the beginning…
There was you.
In the middle
There is you
Are you walking in the magnitude of the First Words spoken over you?
Or have you swallowed the world's cynicism and scepticism
Have you digested the 'isms'
And grown so fat in logic and intellect
That mundane living is your new excellence?
'Knowledge is power'
But what use is knowledge if it never encounters?
If it is never engaged? If it never experiences life on a level that leads to failure, to disappointment, to grief?
Such knowledge is dormant and asleep

You cannot simply read your way to realising your dreams
You must walk. You must run. You must fall, get up and crawl till you can walk again.
But if you must read your way to realising your dreams, go back to the Beginning.
Go back to the magnitude of the First Words spoken over you.
Go back to **Eden**.